AMIGOS

Senior Authors
Carl B. Smith
Virginia A. Arnold

Linguistics Consultant
Ronald Wardhaugh

Macmillan Publishing Co., Inc.
New York
Collier Macmillan Publishers
London

Copyright © 1983 Macmillan Publishing Co., Inc.

All rights reserved. No part of this book may be reproduced or transmitted in any form or by any means, electronic or mechanical, including photocopying, recording, or by any information storage and retrieval system, without permission in writing from the Publisher.

This work is also published together with other works in a single volume under the title: *Opening Doors,* copyright © 1983 Macmillan Publishing Co., Inc. Parts of this work were published in earlier editions of SERIES r.

Macmillan Publishing Co., Inc.
866 Third Avenue
New York, New York 10022
Collier Macmillan Canada, Inc.

Printed in the United States of America
ISBN 0-02-131950-2
9 8 7 6 5 4 3 2 1

ACKNOWLEDGMENTS

The publisher gratefully acknowledges permission to reprint the following copyrighted material:

"The Donkey Knows," adapted from "I Think I Know," from *Fried Onions and Marshmallows* by Sally Melcher Jarvis. Copyright © 1968 by Sally Melcher Jarvis. By permission of Parents' Magazine Press.

"I Woke Up One Morning," from *A Rumbudgin of Nonsense* by Arnold Spilka. Copyright © 1970 by Arnold Spilka. Reprinted by permission of Arnold Spilka.

"I wonder how it feels to fly . . . ," adapted from *The Turquoise Horse* edited by Flora Hood. Copyright © 1972 by Flora Hood. Reprinted by permission of G.P. Putnam's Sons and Curtis Brown, Ltd.

"If I Were a . . . ," from *The Rose On My Cake* by Karla Kuskin. Copyright © 1964 by Karla Kuskin. By permission of Harper & Row, Publishers, Inc.

"Look," from *All That Sunlight* by Charlotte Zolotow. Copyright © 1967 by Charlotte Zolotow. By permission of Harper & Row, Publishers, Inc.

"Silly Sam," adapted from *Silly Sam* by Leonore Klein. Copyright © 1969 by Scholastic Magazines, Inc. Reprinted by permission of Scholastic Magazines, Inc.

"Things in the Pool," from *Little Raccoon and Poems From The Woods* by Lilian Moore. Copyright © 1975 by Lilian Moore. By permission of McGraw-Hill Book Company.

"Things That Go Together," from *Just Think!* by Betty Miles and Joan Blos. Copyright © 1971 by Betty Miles. Reprinted by permission of Alfred A. Knopf, Inc.

"Tree House," from *Where the Sidewalk Ends* by Shel Silverstein. Copyright © 1974 by Shel Silverstein. By permission of Harper & Row, Publishers, Inc.

Illustrations: Ray Cruz, pp. 4-7; Sal Murdocca, pp. 10-11; Bob Shein, pp. 12-21; Don Leake, pp. 24-39; Jerry Zimmerman, pp. 40-41; Tom Cook, pp. 50-51; Tom Herbert, pp. 52-63; Liebert Studios, pp. 64-65; Kevin Callahan, pp. 66-85; Les Gray, pp. 88-101; Frank Bozzo, pp. 102-103. **Photographs:** James Foote, pp. 38, 41, 46, 47; Beryl Goldberg, p. 45 (left); T. Crissinger, p. 45 (right).

Contents

Introduction to AMIGOS 9

Who Is So Pretty?, *a poem by Elizabeth Coatsworth* 10

Mouse Wants a Friend, *a story by Helen Piers*
    Who Can Be a Friend? 12
    Mouse Finds a Friend 17

SKILLS: Write a Word (Short Vowels) 22

The Happy Woman, *a story by Dina Anastasio*
    The School Bus 24
    A Sad Day 27
    The Old Woman at School 34

The Wheels of the Bus Go Round and Round,
    an anonymous poem 40

SKILLS: Suzy's Day (Sequence of Events) 42

In School Again, an essay by Sally R. Bell 44

I Wish I Had a Diamond, a poem by Richard Ulloa 50

The House in the Woods, a story by Judith Adams
    A Place for Things 52
    The Green Rock 55
    A Surprise 59

Slow Pokes, a poem by Laura Arlon 64

Izzy, a story by Jeanette McNeely
    Where Is Izzy? 66
    Hal Runs Fast 73
    Hal Finds Izzy 77
    Hal and Izzy 81

SKILLS: Word Surprise (Rhyming Words) 86

Here I Come, a story by Judith Adams
    A Day for the Park 88
    One, Two, Three 92
    That Red Hat Again 96

The Secret Place, a poem by Dorothy Aldis 102

Conclusion for AMIGOS 104

Word List 105

7

AMIGOS

"Amigos" is a word
that says friends.
Who are your friends?
What do you and
your friends like to do?

As you read "Amigos,"
see if the friends
do things that you do.

Who Is So Pretty?

Skitter, skatter,
Leap and squeak!
We've been dancing
Half the week.

Under the sofa,
Along the shelf,
Every mouse
Is wild as an elf.

Big round ear
And bright black eye,
Nimble and natty,
Limber and spry—

Who is so pretty,
Who is so neat,
As a little mouse dancing
On little gray feet?

—Elizabeth Coatsworth

Mouse Wants a Friend

Helen Piers

**Part One
Who Can Be a Friend?**

Mouse wants a friend.
He wants a friend
who can run and jump.

Can he be a friend?
No.
He can't run and jump.
He likes to sit and look.

Can he be a friend?
No.
He can't run and jump.
He likes to fly.

Mouse wants a friend
who does not sit and look.
He wants a friend
who does not fly.
Mouse wants a friend
who can run and jump.

Part Two
Mouse Finds a Friend

Can he be a friend?
No.
He can't run.
He can jump.
But he jumps high.
He jumps too high.

Can he be a friend?
No.
He can't run and jump.
He likes to walk slowly.
He walks too slowly.

Mouse wants to find a friend.
But he does not like
to sit and look.
He can't fly or jump high.
And he does not like
to walk slowly.
Will Mouse
find a friend?

Look!
What is that?

Does she jump up and down?
Yes!

Does she run in and out?
Yes!
Is she the friend Mouse wants?

Yes!

She is a mouse, too.

Write a Word

Look at the letters in the box.
Find the letters that make
the words go with the pictures.
Write the words on your paper.

| a | e | i | o | u |

 1. c <u>a</u> n

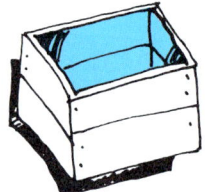 2. b __ x

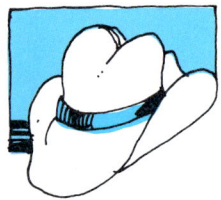 3. h __ t

 4. s __ n

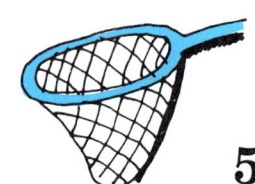 5. n __ t

 6. p __ g

Find the letter that makes a word.
Write the word on your paper.
Then write the sentence.

h a s
| a | u |

1. Kate ___ a bike.

B _ b
| i | o |

2. ___ likes to ride.

l _ t
| e | u |

3. Will Kate ___ Bob ride the bike?

w _ ll
| o | i |

4. Yes, Kate ___ let Bob ride.

b _ s
| u | e |

5. Kate rides the ___ .

The Happy Woman

Dina Anastasio

**Part One
The School Bus**

I went to school on a bus.
My friends went on the bus, too.
We liked to ride
on the school bus.

A happy woman drove the bus.
We liked the happy woman
who drove the bus.
She drove and she sang.
She sang to the birds.
She sang to the dogs.
She sang to my friends.
And we sang, too.

The woman gave funny presents
to my friends and me.
And we gave funny presents
to the woman.

I gave little things,
like a little mouse
and a little car.

She liked the car.
She liked the mouse, too.

Part Two
A Sad Day

One day the happy woman
was not on the bus.

A new woman drove the bus that day.
The new woman was not too happy.

We sang to the new woman.
But she said,
"I don't like that.
You can't do that on the bus."

I said to the new woman,
"Where is my friend
who drove the bus?"

The new woman said,
"She is too old.
She is at home."

"I want to see her.
She is my friend," I said.

So one day I went
to find the old woman.
I went to her house.
The old woman was not there.
But a little girl was there.

I said, "Where is the woman
who likes boys and girls?"

"She is at the park with her dog.
You will find her there,"
said the girl.

I went to the park,
but she was not there.

A woman was there.
But she was not my friend.

So I went home.
"I can't find the happy old woman,"
I said.

I was sad that day.
The old woman was my friend.

Part Three
The Old Woman at School

One day I went to school.
And there was the old woman!

"Are you going to drive the bus?"
I said.
"Are you going to drive
my friends and me home?"

"No," said the woman.
"I can't drive the bus.
But I can do other work.
I will see if I can find
other work here."

I went into school.

"The old woman is here,"
I said to my friends.
"She is here to find work."

My friends said,
"She is too old.
She can't work here."

"She can if she wants to,"
I said.

In school we read,
and we sang.
But the day went slowly.

Then we went to the lunchroom.
And there she was!
The old woman!

"Are you going to work here?"
I said.

"Yes," she said.
"I like it here in the lunchroom.
I can be with my friends."

So the old woman worked
in the lunchroom.
"I like to be
with my friends," she said.
"And they like to be
with me, too."

The Wheels of the Bus

The wheels of the bus go round and round
Round and round, round and round.
The wheels of the bus go round and round
All through the town.

Go Round and Round

The people on the bus go up and down
Up and down, up and down.
The people on the bus go up and down
All through the town.

The kids on the bus go *yakkity-yak*
Yakkity-yak, yakkity-yak.
The kids on the bus go *yakkity-yak*
All through the town.

— *Anonymous*

Suzy's Day

Here is what Suzy does one day.

Read the sentences.
They say what Suzy does.

- Suzy is going to the lunchroom.
- Suzy sits down and looks at pictures.
- Suzy jumps up.

1. On your paper, write the sentence that says what Suzy does first.

2. Write the sentence that says what she does next.

3. Then write the sentence that says what Suzy does last.

In School Again
Sally R. Bell

It is the first day of school.
Boys and girls go to school again.
They see friends.
They work.
There are many things to do.
It is the first day of school.

There are new boys and girls
in the school.
They may not know where to go.
They may be lost in school.
They may not have friends.
They will find new friends.

Other boys and girls help
the new boys and girls.
They will help with the work.
They will be new friends.

There is time to read in school.
There is time to paint.
There is time to play, too.
Boys and girls do many things in school.

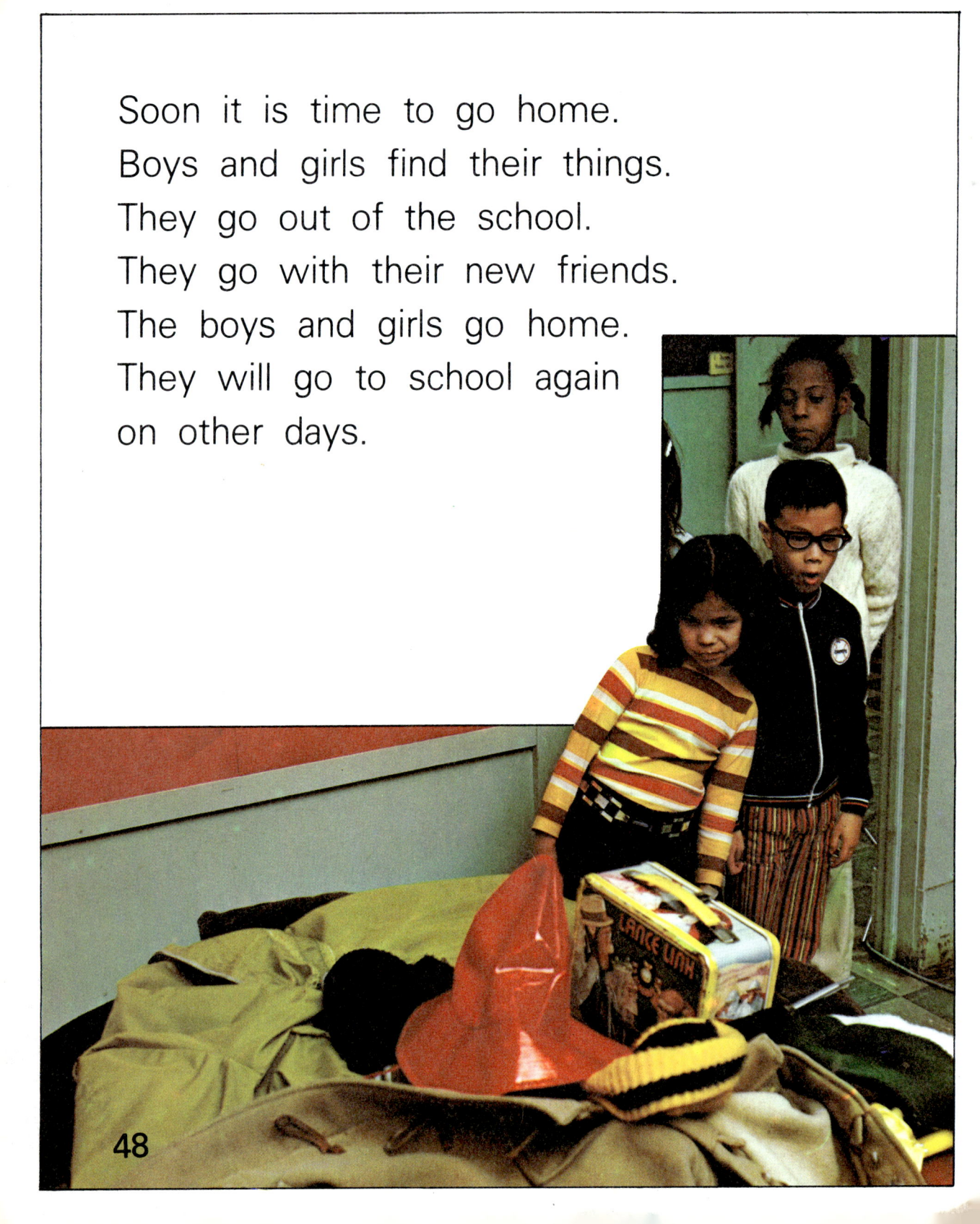

Soon it is time to go home.
Boys and girls find their things.
They go out of the school.
They go with their new friends.
The boys and girls go home.
They will go to school again
on other days.

There will be many things for boys and girls to do. They like to go to school.

I wish I had a diamond
I wish I had a bike
I wish I had a cat
I wish I had a puppy
I wish I had a friend.

—Richard Ulloa
Grade One

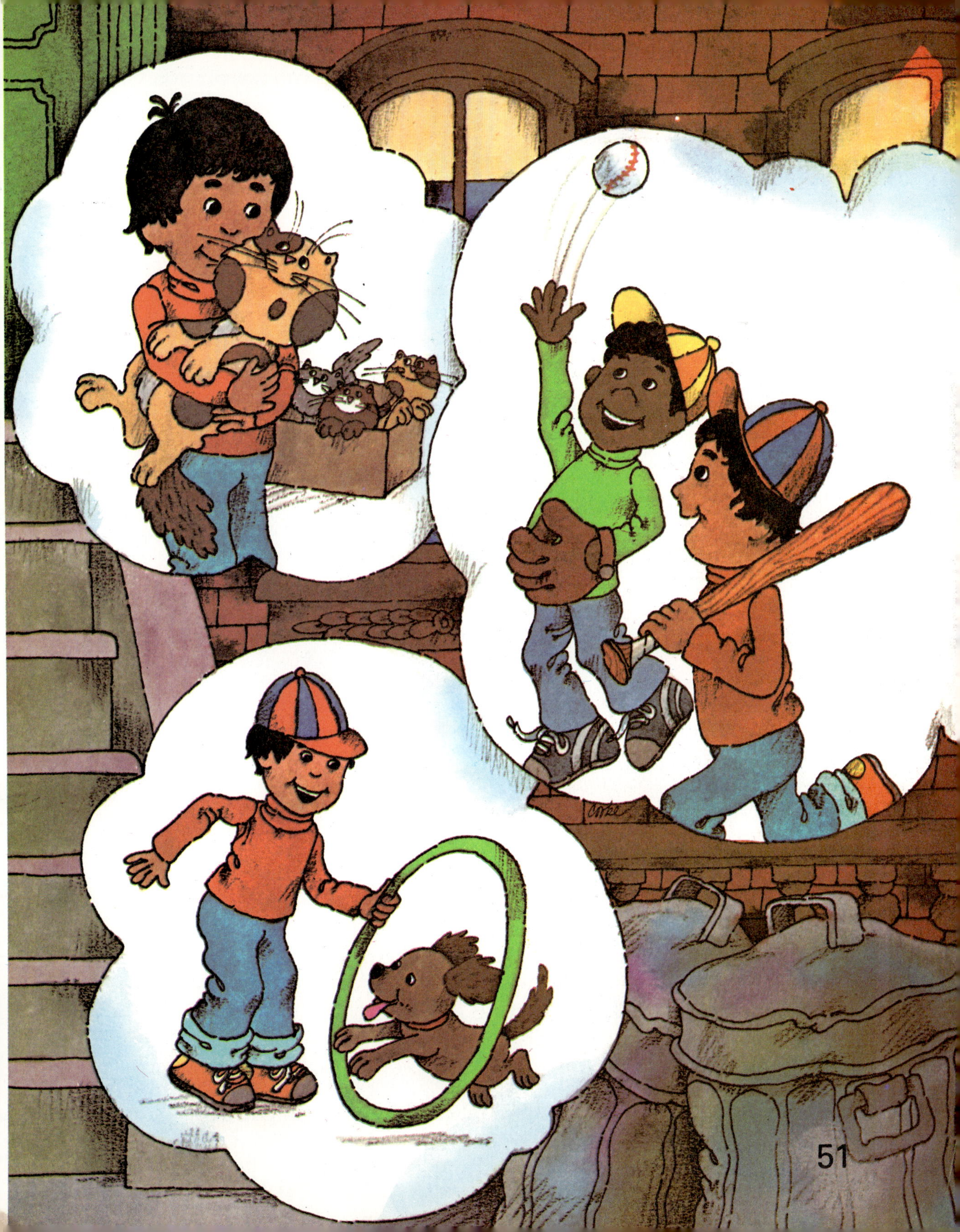

The House in the Woods

Judith Adams

**Part One
A Place for Things**

There was a hill in the woods.
There was a house on the hill.
And there was a man in the house.
The man liked things to be in place.

He liked to know
where to find his hat
and where to find his umbrella.
He liked to know
where to find his other things.

So there was a place for his hat and a place for his umbrella. And there was a place for his other things, too.

"I like to know where things are," said the man.

**Part Two
The Green Rock**

The man was happy with his things.
And he was happy to have a house
in the woods.

One day he went out for a walk
in the woods.
The woods were green.

"What a day!" said the man.

He looked at the woods.
There were birds that sang.
There was a little lake.
There were fish in the lake.

The man saw the birds fly.
And he saw the fish jump.
And he liked what he saw.

Then the man looked down.
And he saw a rock.
It was a green rock,
and he liked it.

"It will go with my things,"
said the man.
"I will find a place for it
if I can."

He looked at the woods.
He saw the fish and the birds.
And he saw his green rock.
The man was happy.

"What a day!" he said.

**Part Three
A Surprise**

"Will my green rock go here?"
said the man.

But the rock looked too big.
It did not go there.

"Will it go here?"

But the rock looked too little.
It did not go there.

"I like this rock," said the man.
"But if there is no place for it,
I can't have it in my house.
Out you go."

But then he looked at the rock.
"What is this?" he said.
"A turtle! A surprise!
A green turtle!
What a surprise!"

"This turtle can be my friend.
Can I find a place for a friend
in my house?"

The man looked at his hat box.
Then he looked at the box
for his other things.

"My hat does not have to have a box," he said.
"It can go with my other things."

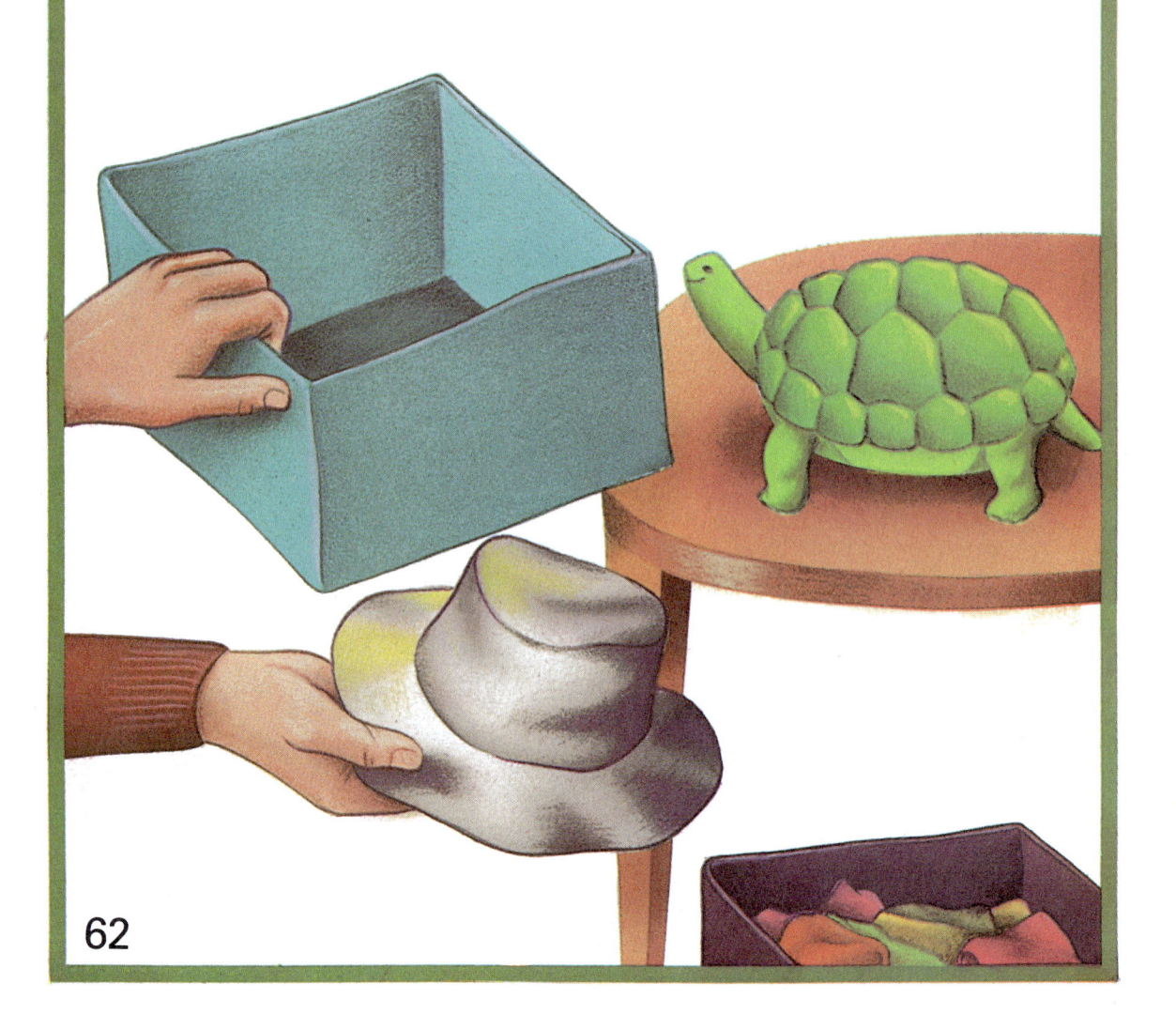

"This box will be for you,"
the man said to the turtle.
"There is a place for my things
and a place for you!"

And the man and the turtle
were happy in the house
on the hill in the woods.

Slow Pokes

Turtles are slow,
As we all know.
But
To them
It is no worry,

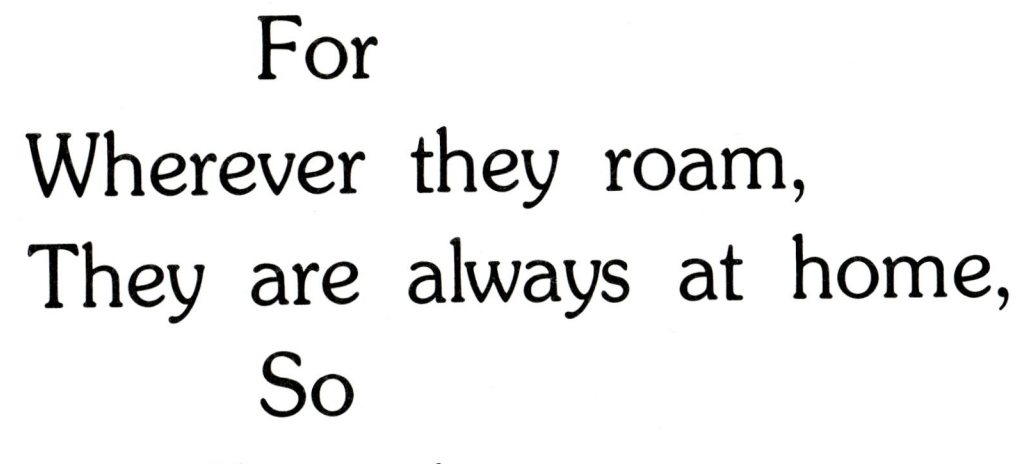

For
Wherever they roam,
They are always at home,
So
They do not
HAVE
To hurry.

— LAURA ARLON

Izzy

Jeannette McNeely

**Part One
Where Is Izzy?**

Hal looked in the box.
Mindy looked, too.

"Izzy was in this box.
He is not here.
Where is Izzy?" said Hal.

"Does your mother know?
Did you ask your mother?"
said Mindy.

"No!" said Hal.
"If I ask my mother, she will want me to do my school work."

"Does your father know?
Did you ask your father?"
Mindy said.

"No!" said Hal.
"If I ask my father, he will want me to paint the house."

"Did you ask that man?" said Mindy.

"No!" said Hal.
"He will want my help."

"Did you ask that woman?"
said Mindy.

"No!
She will want my help, too."

Then Mindy said,
"I know what you can do, Hal.
You can ask and run!"

"Why do you say that?" said Hal.

"If you ask and run,
then you don't have to help,"
said Mindy.

"Yes!" said Hal.
"That is what I will do."
"Hal! Hal!" said Mindy.

But Hal was not there.

**Part Two
Hal Runs Fast**

Hal ran to the house.

He saw his mother.
"Have you seen Izzy?" Hal said as he ran.

"No, Hal, but—"
Hal ran fast.
"Hal!" said his mother.

But he was gone.

He saw his father.

"Have you seen Izzy?"
Hal said as he ran.

"No, Hal.
But—"

Hal ran fast and was gone.

Hal saw the man.
"Have you seen Izzy?" said Hal as he ran.

"No," said the man.
Then he looked up.
"Hal—"

But Hal ran too fast for the man.

Hal saw the woman.
"Have you seen Izzy?" said Hal.

"No," said the woman.
"Is—?"

But Hal ran fast and was gone.

**Part Three
Hal Finds Izzy**

Hal saw the mail carrier.
"Have you seen Izzy?" said Hal.

"Who is Izzy?"
said the mail carrier.

"Izzy is my lizard,"
Hal said.

"He is, is he?"
the mail carrier said.

"Yes, Izzy is my lizard.
But where is he?" Hal said.

"Hal, come here,"
said the mail carrier.
"Is this lizard Izzy?"

"Yes!" said Hal.
"This is Izzy!"

Part Four
Hal and Izzy

"I see you found your lizard," said the woman.
"I wanted to tell you, but you ran too fast."

"I see you found your lizard,"
said the man.
"I wanted to tell you,
but you ran too fast."

"I see you found your lizard,"
said Mindy.
"I wanted to tell you,
but you ran too fast."

Hal and the mail carrier
laughed.

Hal saw his father.

"I see you found Izzy,"
his father said.
"I wanted to tell you, but—"

"I know.
I ran too fast."
Hal laughed.

Hal went to the house.

"I see you found Izzy," said his mother.

"I know," Hal said. "You wanted to tell me, but I ran too fast."

"No," said his mother. "I wanted to tell you to do your school work!"

"Mother!" said Hal.

Then he looked at Izzy, and he laughed.

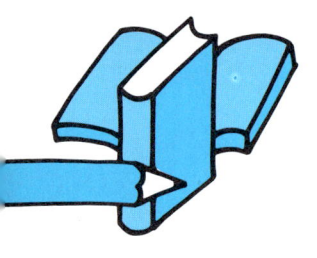

Word Surprise

Find the letter or letters in a box to make the picture word.
Write the word on your paper.

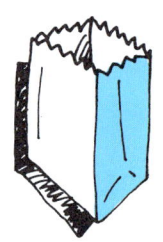

| b | t | k |

1. _b_ ag

| fl | dr | pr |

2. ___ ag

| r | m | s |

3. ___ ip

| fr | dr | sl |

4. ___ ip

| s | b | r |

5. ___ ide

| sl | br | gr |

6. ___ ide

Find the letter or letters in a box
to make a new word.
Write the sentence on your paper.

1. I see a bat.
   Can it fly into a hat? | h | s | t |

2. Go down on your sled.
   Then come to __ed. | m | g | b |

3. See the rain drip.
   Don't you __ip. | sl | pr | fr |

4. Have a ride.
   Come to the __ide. | fl | sl | fr |

5. See that man in red.
   He looks like __ed. | Fl | Pr | Fr |

6. Get a grip.
   Do a __ip. | fr | fl | pr |

87

Here I Come

Judith Adams

Part One
A Day for the Park

Debbie and Ann are friends.
If it does not rain,
the girls like to go to the park.

One day Ann said,
"Debbie, Debbie, come on out.
This is a day for the park.
That's the place to go."

Debbie looked out.
"It looks like a day for the park,"
she said.
"I'll be out.
Wait for me."

ONE WAY

"Ann, wait for me!"
It was a boy.

"Who is that?" said Debbie.

"That's Jay," said Ann.
"His mother and my mother are friends."

The boy ran up to the girls.

"Do you want to come to the park?" said Ann.

"That's the place to be on a day like this," said Jay. "I'll come."

"Run and hide," said Ann.
"Then I'll find you."

"I like to hide," said Debbie.
"Come on, Jay."

"I like to hide, too," said Jay.
"Wait and see.
I'll hide so Ann can't find me!"

Jay and Debbie ran to hide.

**Part Two
One, Two, Three**

One.
Two.
Three.
Here I come!

Ann looked for Jay and Debbie.
She saw a box.
She looked in.
But she did not see Jay or Debbie.

Then she saw a red thing.

"That's a red hat," said Ann.
"Jay had his red hat on.
That's Jay!"

"I see you, Jay.
Come out.
Come out,
and I'll look for Debbie,"
said Ann.

"I saw you peek," said Jay.
"You saw me run and hide.
That's what you did."

"I did not peek," Ann said.
"I saw your red hat.
But hide if you want to.
I'll call one, two, three.
Then I'll look for you."

"Wait here," said Jay as he ran.
"And don't peek!"

One.
Two.
Three.
Here I come.

Part Three
That Red Hat Again

Ann looked in the box again.
But no one was there.
She looked and looked.
She saw a big rock.
Then she saw the red hat move.

It was Jay!
Ann didn't see Debbie.

"Come out, Jay," Ann said.

"You said one, two, three too fast."
Jay said.
"So I didn't hide where I wanted to.
And that's why you found me.
I want to hide again."

Ann was not happy with Jay.
But she said, "Hide again.
You can hide where you want to.
Let's see if I can find you."

One.
Two.
Three.
Here I come.

Ann looked and looked.
Then she looked up.
She saw a red thing move.
It was Jay with his red hat again.

But Ann didn't call Jay.

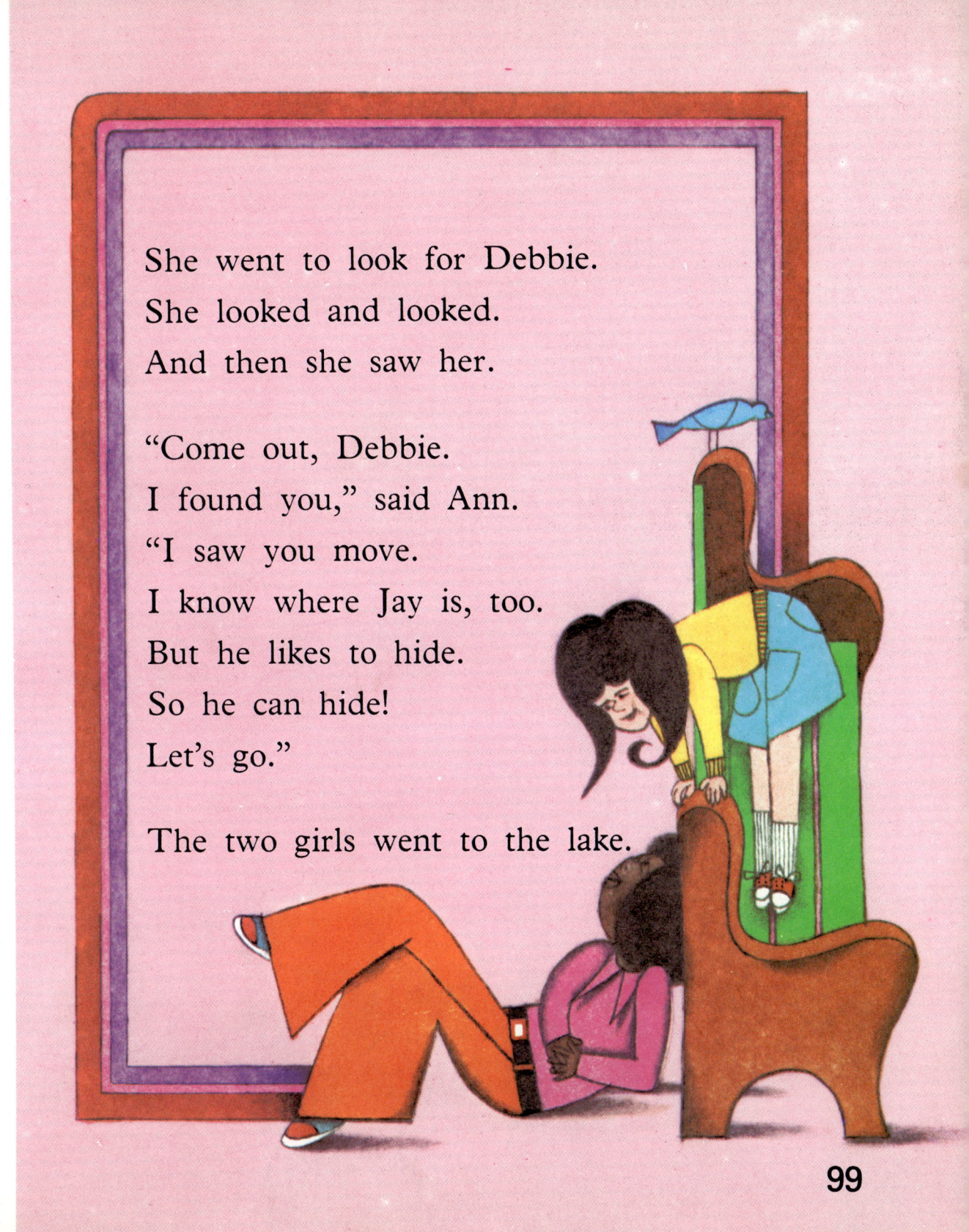

She went to look for Debbie.
She looked and looked.
And then she saw her.

"Come out, Debbie.
I found you," said Ann.
"I saw you move.
I know where Jay is, too.
But he likes to hide.
So he can hide!
Let's go."

The two girls went to the lake.

"Where is Ann?" said Jay.
"I don't want to wait here.
I'll see where she is."

Jay went to the lake.
"Ann," he said.
"I wanted you to find me."

"I did," said Ann.
"But you didn't like it.
So I let you hide."

Jay was happy to be
with his friends again.
He likes to hide sometimes.
But he didn't hide again that day!

The Secret Place

Halfway up a certain tree
There's a place belongs to me,
Two branches make a little chair
And I like it sitting there.

I like it.
And it's a secret too.
No grownup guesses where I go.
And if he should, and climbed to it—
He would not fit, he would not fit!

—DOROTHY ALDIS

AMIGOS

The friends in "Amigos"
did many things.
They worked and played.

Thinking About "Amigos"

1. Why did Mouse want to find a friend?
2. Why did the little girl want to find her friend who drove the bus?
3. What will the new boys and girls do in school?
4. What things did the friends in "Amigos" do that you do, too?

Word List

9.	Amigos	18.	slowly
	friends	20.	she
	as		yes
12.	part	22.	write
	mouse		letters
	wants		make
	be		pictures
	no		paper
17.	finds		
	high		

To the Teacher: The words listed beside the page numbers above are instructional-vocabulary words introduced in *Amigos*.

23. sentence
24. happy
    woman
    school
    went
    liked
25. drove
    sang
26. gave
27. day
    was
    new
28. said
29. old
    her
30. there

34. going
    drive
35. other
    work
    here
38. lunchroom
39. worked
    they
42. Suzy's
43. first
    next
    last
44. again
    many
45. know
46. help

47. time
    play
48. soon
    their
49. for
52. place
53. his

55. green
    rock
    were
56. looked
    saw
59. surprise
60. this

61. turtle
66. Izzy
    Hal
    Mindy
67. mother
    ask
68. father
73. fast
    seen
74. gone
77. mail
    carrier
78. lizard
81. four
    found
    wanted
    tell
83. laughed

88. Debbie
    Ann
    that's
    I'll
    wait
90. Jay
94. peek
96. move
97. didn't
    let's
101. sometimes
104. thinking
     about

Word List

9.	if	43.	sentences
12.	friend	48.	days
16.	not	73.	ran
19.	find	86.	picture
22.	box	87.	rain
23.	letter	91.	hide
	makes	93.	thing
29.	want		had
37.	read	101.	let
		104.	played

To the Teacher: The children should be able to independently identify the applied-skills words listed beside the page numbers above by using previously taught phonics skills or by recognizing derived forms of words previously introduced.